Bobby Gilliam,
Brave and Strong

Written by
Carolyn Byers Ruch

Illustrated by
Josh Manges

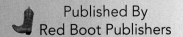 Published By
Red Boot Publishers

Dear Parent, Teacher, or Trusted Caregiver,

We wish we could ignore it. We wish it would go away. But currently 1 out of every 4 girls and 1 out of every 6 boys will be sexually violated by their eighteenth birthday.

Although we need to teach children about strangers, it is not the stranger who is the biggest threat to our kids. Ninety percent of children who are molested are violated by someone they know and trust—neighbors, babysitters, coaches, teachers, doctors, faith leaders, friends, nuclear family members, extended family members, teens, and even other children. It is a grave mistake to believe sexual abuse could never happen to a child we love.

We must teach our children what sexual abuse is and what they should do if they encounter it. It is vital that they know they can always come to us—no matter who was involved.

This is why we created *Bobby Gilliam, Brave and Strong*, a book for boys, and *Ana's Song*, a book for girls. Our mission is to help you build a bridge of communication between yourself and the kids you love and long to protect. We want your children to be prepared should anyone show them inappropriate images, speak to them in an inappropriate manner, touch them in an inappropriate manner, or perhaps ask your child to touch them in an inappropriate manner.

Please, read our stories to the children in your care. Begin the conversation. Build the bridge. Break the silence. So your children, like Bobby, the hero in *Bobby Gilliam, Brave and Strong*, and Ana, the heroine in *Ana's Song*, can be free to be everything they were created to be.

With heartfelt gratitude for your desire to protect children,

Carolyn and Josh

* For discussion questions and more information, please visit **RiseAndShineMovement.org**

To the men and boys who have faced "aliens."

You are brave.

You are strong.

And to Cec Murphey,
for lighting the path toward healing
for the men we love.
(Menshatteringthesilence.blogspot.com)

Carolyn Byers Ruch

To all the boys who
have experienced pain and
have continued on, stay strong.

Josh Manges

The sun rose over the city just as it did every other morning. Cars honked, trains roared, and Bobby Gilliam snoozed beneath his covers, still dreaming of yesterday's fun.

He had played at the park all day, pretending to be anyone he wanted to be.

First he was a pilot, flying jet planes, soaring through the air. "Fasten your seatbelts. Bumpy ride ahead."

Next he was a surfer, skimming across the waves, conquering wide oceans. "Hang loose, dude!"

Then he raced toward the wide-open field, mostly because Bobby Gilliam wanted to grow up to be a soccer player—just like his dad.

The score was tied, five to five. Bobby shot. He scored! The whistle blew. The crowd roared!

"We won!" the team cheered and lifted him high in the air.
"Speech, Bobby. Speech!"

"We won't forget this day," Bobby said. "Our team was brave. Our team was strong."

Suddenly, the clouds parted. A flashing spaceship spun to earth. The door flew open. A man in a spacesuit floated toward Bobby. "Come, Bobby Gilliam, come with me. On my planet the sun always shines. Fun never ends. And if you play secret games with me, I will give you the universe. You will grow up to be everything I want you to be."

Something in the spaceman's eyes—something about the secret games he wanted to play—made Bobby feel funny, a little sick in his stomach. "No, I don't think so, Mr. Spaceman. I don't want to play. Besides, when I grow up, I want to play soccer just like my dad."

Then the spacesuit burst apart. An alien appeared. He was green. He was ugly. His red eye blazed and shifted to each team member, causing them all to disappear, leaving Bobby to face the alien.

Alone.

Ooze flowed from his nostrils. He screeched from between his fangs. "Come with me and play my secret games, or you will never see your parents again."

The alien crawled toward him.

"No!" Bobby yelled. "No! I told you, I don't want to play." And he ran away.

Then he heard his father's voice, "Rise and shine, Bobby. Wake up. You're dreaming."

Bobby's eyes popped open. "Dad, an alien wanted to play a secret game, but I said no. He got mad and said if I didn't play with him, I would never see you or Mom again."

"Nobody has the right to make you play games you don't want to," his father said. "I'm glad you told the alien no and didn't believe his lies. You were brave. You were strong. Now come out from under those covers and feel the sunlight on your face."

"Do you feel safe now?" his father asked.

"Yeah, and my stomach doesn't hurt either."

"Good. I want you always to feel safe, just like you do now."

Bobby smiled.

"Remember, God makes the sun rise each day for you. He wants you to imagine, pretend, and play so you can grow up to be all you were created to be. I don't want you to be afraid, his father continued. "But there's something I must tell you, something you need to know. One day, you might face a different kind of alien—a real person. A man or a woman who might ask you to look at pictures or videos you shouldn't see or to play secret games."

"What kind of pictures or videos?" Bobby asked. "What kind of secret games?"

"Pictures or videos of other people with their clothes off. It's called pornography, Bobby. It's not good for you or me. Or they might want to play touching games and touch your body where your swimsuit covers, or they might ask you to touch their body where their swimsuit covers. Those body parts are private. No one is allowed to touch you there. No one is allowed to ask you to touch them there."

Bobby scrunched his nose. "That's gross!"

"Yes, it is. But if someone wants you to look at pornography or play these games, yell, 'No!' Run! Tell me, tell Mom, or tell another adult. It's our job to protect you. Understand?"

Bobby nodded. "I'm going to yell no, run, and tell—just like I did to the scary alien."

"Exactly! Now get dressed. Uncle Ralph is coming over for burgers tonight while Mom's at work. We'll have fun, just us dudes. No aliens."

Bobby smiled. "And I won't be afraid."

"You're right, Bobby. You don't need to fear. Because, Bobby Gilliam, you are brave. You are strong."

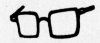

Bobby raced to get dressed. He loved Uncle Ralph. Uncle Ralph was fun. Uncle Ralph was cool. And Bobby loved to hang out with him, even though he wasn't his real uncle. Uncle Ralph was his dad's friend.

Bobby spent the afternoon getting his toys ready to play with his father and Uncle Ralph. First they would play cops and robbers. The good guys would win.

Next, they would build enormous buildings with giant blocks and battle ferocious monsters. The city would be saved!

Mom left for work, and Uncle Ralph came over. They played cops and robbers for a while. But then Bobby's dad stepped outside to grill some burgers.

Uncle Ralph had a new idea. "Bobby," he said. "Remember that video we watched on my cell phone, where the aliens took over the universe? You know, the one I told you not to tell your dad about, because he doesn't like aliens? You didn't tell your dad our secret, did you?"

"No way!" said Bobby.

"Well, I have a new video today. You're going to love it. And, Bobby, we won't tell your dad about this one either. It will be our secret."

The video began to play. There weren't aliens in this video, but there were people. The people were kissing. Bobby hated kissing.

Bobby looked at his blocks. "Uncle Ralph, want to build a skyscraper?"

"Pay attention!" said Uncle Ralph. "You're going to like this video. All the big kids do."

Bobby looked at the screen and saw pictures he didn't want to see. Pictures his father had just warned him about. The people in the video started taking off their clothes.

Bobby's stomach ached. He felt sad and confused. He was curious, but he still didn't want to see it. Now he felt really sick.

Suddenly, Bobby remembered his father's words about secret games and pictures of naked people. *Yell no!* he thought. *Run. Tell.*

But Bobby didn't want to hurt Uncle Ralph's feelings. He was afraid.

Then he remembered, *Bobby Gilliam, you are brave. You are strong.*

Bobby got an idea.

"Uncle Ralph, I feel sick." Bobby raced to the bathroom and locked the door.

Uncle Ralph knocked on the bathroom door. "You okay, Bobby? Remember, this video is our secret. I'll be really mad at you if you tell your dad. I'll never play with you again."

"What video?" Bobby's dad had walked in the door just in time to hear Uncle Ralph's words. "And you're right, Ralph, you will never play with my son again. Leave. Now."

Uncle Ralph grabbed his cell phone and hurried out the door.

Bobby's dad knocked on the bathroom door. "Bobby, you okay?"

Bobby opened the door and told his father about the video,
the alien video, and the secrets Uncle Ralph told him to keep.

Bobby's dad knelt down. He held Bobby's shoulders with his big, gentle
hands. "Bobby, look at me. Look into my eyes. I believe you. This was not
your fault. Uncle Ralph shouldn't have shown you those videos or asked
you to keep secrets from me. I'm so glad you told me. I am proud of you!
You are brave. You are strong."

Then Bobby and his dad made burgers, built tall buildings, battled ferocious monsters, and saved the city.

The sun rose over the city just as it did every other morning. Horns honked, trains roared, and Bobby Gilliam, now a grown man, woke up and got ready for work.

But he didn't grow up to fly airplanes. Flying made his stomach ache.

He didn't surf the big wide oceans. The oceans were too far away.

He didn't become a soccer player, because there was something he liked to do more.

So what did Bobby grow up to be?

He grew up to be an architect, to design beautiful buildings and ginormous skyscrapers.

And Bobby Gilliam, brave and strong, grew up to be a daddy just like his dad. Free to be everything he was created to be.

28024525R00022

Made in the USA
Middletown, DE
30 December 2015